Always Assume an Attitude of Confidence: Never Feel Intimidated or Apologetic

Category: Business & Economics

Author: Bob Oros

Publisher: Bob Oros Publishing

ISBN: 978-1-387-20087-0

Copyright 2017

Description: You want to portray confidence every time you talk to a prospect or client. If you don't believe in yourself, no one else will. It's important you communicate with clients and prospects in a manner where you feel and know that your services can benefit them and that you have the knowledge and resources solve their problems and answer their questions.

Key words: food sales jobs, job in sales, sales manager training, manufacturing sales training, wholesale sales training, distributor sales training, food service sales, sales coaching, sales techniques, motivating sales people, sales course, online sales training,

ISBN 978-1-387-20087-0

1. Why should you display an attitude of confidence?

Always assume an attitude of confidence and purpose and never apologize for making the call.

There is a psychological law that makes a person respond to the attitude and action expressed by another person. There is nothing mysterious about it, except the results that come when you put this law into effect.

Everyone wants to do the appropriate thing. Everyone wants to "rise to the occasion." We have an unconscious urge to "live up to" the expectations others have of us, or to "live down" to them. If you see that your customer or prospect is busy when you first walk into their office or warehouse do not apologize for interrupting. What will go through their mind if you do? "If you see I am busy, why are you bothering me?"

If you decide beforehand that a certain customer is going to be difficult to deal with, chances are you will approach them in a hostile manner, ready to fight. When you do this, you literally set the stage for them to act on. He or she rises to the occasion. They act the part that you have set for them to act, and you come away convinced that they really are a "tough customer," without ever realizing that your own actions and attitudes helped make them one.

In dealing with your customers, you see your own attitudes reflected back to you in their behavior. When you smile, the person in front of you smiles. When you frown, the person frowns. When you shout, the person shouts back.

Not taking yourself too seriously and acknowledging your faults and mistakes actually shows your customers that you are confident. Seeing someone you admire do something clumsy or stupid will make you like them more. When you show others that you don't take yourself too seriously it makes them fee closer to you. We like confident, self assured people, however, the truly self confident person doesn't need to let the world know how great they are.

Here is a way to have your customers perceive you as confident and enthusiastic. The most effective for making a favorable first impression is the easiest thing to do: smile. Four things are accomplished when you smile - acceptance, enthusiasm, happiness and, most importantly, confidence.

You are in control! You have the power to control the customers reaction. This takes practice, but the results are amazing

----

Comments:

It is important to forget what just happened at the last call, good or bad, and what you are going to do after the one you are at. Live in the moment, focusing all your attention on this one person. Bring you smile when you enter. Be a good listener. You may be the best thing that has happened to him all day.

Jim Ruth

As salespeople we are professionals and we should never let a customer take that away from us. Enthusiasm, confidence and a positive attitude should always be a part of our calls. If the day wears on you and each call begins to sound like "You really don't want to buy from me," take a break, do something else, it's not going to get better if you don't do something about it? If you are having one of those days end it at an account that respects and admires you

and that says thank you. If you go home with the wrong attitude it will start your next day off quickly in the same wrong direction.

David Vize

If a customer is too busy to see you or does not want to see you apologizing for the interruption is not going to hurt anything. You will still be shut down. And, as previously mentioned, you may gain a little respect. The next time you approach them at least they know in advance that you are sensitive to their wishes and will not be pushy with them. This could make them less defensive and more agreeable to giving you a little of their time.

Crocker Smith

Showing confidence lets the buyer now that you mean business. You know what you're talking about and you know what your doing. It shows that your not there just to waste time and can earn you respect, not only from a potential client but anyone in general.

David Bradley

You have probably had days that begin with you feeling great. As the day progresses, however, your feeling of well-being starts to slip away. By day's end, you are glad it is over. If you have had this experience, you are normal. However, even on down days, you have some control. Your control begins when you decide that YOU are responsible for the attitude you display. I strongly believe that your attitude affects everyone that makes contact with you either in person or over the telephone. Your attitude is not only reflected by your tone of voice but also by the way you stand or sit, and by your facial expressions. You have the choice to reflect a positive attitude or your can go with a less desirable choice.

Yessie Narvaez

We need to have confidence before we walk through the door. If the person on the other side of the desk senses that we are not confident, even a little, they will not have much confidence in us. As far as apologizing goes, it's somewhere in between. We need to acknowledge they may be busy and we appreciate the time they are giving us, but we do not need to apologize for doing our job. As salespeople that's what we do, call on people, and at times they are busy and at other times they are not.

Brandon Sanchez

I've noticed this myself when I go to do a sales call. When I smile and at least act like I'm interested in being there, they are much more receptive and friendly. I also have a comment regarding the comment that is listed. You may feel that apologizing is a sign of showing respect but ask yourself this: Why am I going to apologize for doing my job? There are better things to say then 'I'm sorry for interrupting your busy schedule.' Instead, try "I see that your busy so I'll be brief." It gives the recognition that they are a busy person but you're not apologizing for doing your job.

Matthew Thacker

I agree with Linda that acknowledging a person is busy is a show of respect and that you value their time as much as they do. I appreciate the same courtesy when I am in the middle of something that has a deadline or is of need of immediate attention. When someone is in depth with a project I feel their mind is focused on the task at hand. The majority of what I am trying to say to them is half heard and as the old saying goes "In one ear and out the other." I do agree that attitudes are reflected by others. Reflections of actions begin as early as childhood and continue to develop through out our lives. The best example is when a child is upset and yells or raises their voice they are provoking the parent into displaying the same behavior or action but having the attitude of confidence and control will be detected and the poor behavior will circumcise.

Carla McCrea

You want to portray confidence every time you talk to a prospect or client because if you don't believe in yourself , no one else will. It's important you communicate with clients and prospects in a manner where you feel and know that your services can benefit them and that you have the knowledge and resources solve their problems and answer their questions. If you come across as clueless and unsure of yourself, they will either a) not buy from you, or b) walk all over you

Marquesa Ortega

You ever find yourself driving to work in the mornings, trying to dodge the red lights, cursing at drivers going slower than you? Are you going 80 mph answering emails, listening to voice mails, trying to type, drive and talk while behind the wheel? This all leads to your attitude that slaps your customer in the face on your first call of the day. Wake up 10 or 30 minutes earlier and get a head start. Have all your paperwork ready the night before. I devote one day to get totally organized (usually it's on the weekend when I have time) creating my weekly specials, getting show invitations ready. Not by just filling them out, but with a cover letter, a real nice presentation. I also go through all the trade magazines and make copies for my customers.

Also when the brokers come by with coupons I sort them out by customer, fill them out for them with the appropriate invoices. I may not be the highest in sales, but I try to give my customers something different than the usual sales rep. Quality over quantity sometimes is best.

Trip English

I agree with everything in this section except the part about not apologizing if you see your customer is busy and you are interrupting them. To me it is a sign of respect and a sign that you are aware of the situation they are in and not ignoring it. I believe that one could still show confidence and acknowledge someone's busy schedule.

Linda Cassell

2. How many calls should you be making?

A marketing company did a direct mail campaign to homes in a large city making a special price offer on a product and kept track of the results. They mailed to 50,000 homes in one section of the city, 100,000 homes in another section, and then 250,000 homes in another section.

The results were different than expected on a response rate per thousand.

The 100,000 mailing brought more returns per 1,000 than the 50,000.

The 250,000 mailing brought more returns per 1,000 than the 100,000.

In other words, results per thousand INCREASED as the mailings became larger. Here's why: When you advertise to a few people they read what you have to say and either act on it or very soon forget all about it. When you advertise something to practically everybody in a community, people not only individually read what you have to say but they talk about it to other people – and that is what gets results.

The same principle works in personal selling. The more people you ask to buy the better your closing ratio will be.

Here is another good example making more calls. A friend of mine told me about the time he was a national sales manager for a pharmaceutical company and had the challenge of getting his sales people to make more calls.

While thinking about how to approach his sales team with the challenge of making more calls he phoned one of his friends, an up and coming physician who worked for a new service that makes house calls on patients, to ask his opinion about one of the products he was selling. When the doctor came to the phone he said "I just can't talk to you now, call me at nine-thirty tonight." When the sales manager telephoned that night the doctor apologized. "I'm sorry I couldn't talk to you today, it's just one of my regular days – I made house calls on thirty-four patients, had an hour and a half of consultation at my office and delivered two babies."

My friend said he was not at a loss for an interesting opening statement when he began his speech at their national sales meeting.

Are you familiar with The Rule of Seven? It started back in Hollywood during the Great Depression, when people had limited money and shouldn't have been spending it on movies when they had so many other, more pressing needs. The marketing folks discovered that to motivate a person to attend a show, they had to hit those people at least 7 times in a short period of time. Then they showed up at the box office. We've got to do the same thing with our personal selling. When you target a new account, try making seven calls with short intervals in between.

"Familiarity breeds contempt," is commonly accepted, but it is not true. A study conducted in 1982 published in the Journal of Experimental Social Psychology, by R. L. Moreland and R. B. Zajonc, said that repeated exposure to any stimulus leads to a greater appreciation and liking. This is great news for us in sales and marketing. Exposure and repetition can only increase sales.

As a sales person there are several things you can do on the personal level that will make you unique. The first thing you can do is show up.

Comments:

It has been proven many times over that the number of calls you make equals a certain number of sales. The key to this is time management. I found myself with a number of accounts and there was no more time to make call or add more business. Then my manager asked me to layout all my calls on a monthly calendar. As I started to do as he requested I knew he was wrong and this was just a stupid waste of my time. As I got to the last week I found I had time! I have tested this theory many times over with the same results. If you have 100 accounts that you are working, your days are full, no time left to do more. If you lost 25 of those accounts within a short period of time those 75 accounts will fill your days, no time left to do more." In sales numbers are key, but time management is the tool that allows you to do those numbers.

David Vize

Take care of your established customer's needs first and make as many calls as possible the rest of the time. What else is there to do?

Crocker Smith

The more sales call you make the more closes you are going to have! The more people you get out and see the more closes you going to have. So ask yourself, how much money do I want to make? If your answer is a lot, get off your butt and go make it!

David Bradley

The more sales calls you make, the bigger and better the opportunities become that you run into. I always try to have an objective or a point when I am making my calls, whether it is in person or by phone. I have found that by having 1 question I usually open the door for all kinds of discussion of what is going on internally with that client's company. It grows my relationship with the client as well. I have a few prospects that I know have no "needs" that I can assist them with now, but they may know someone that does…. I still continually check in with these people for our relationship growth. If they ever have a need I am sure they will allow me to help, and they will most defiantly refer me to a friend! Word of mouth can be your best friend or worst nightmare! In summary you can never make enough calls, there are always more prospects to call on!

Brooke Knight

Sales are all about putting ourselves in front of our prospects as much as possible. At times it may seem like we are being "annoying" by visiting them so often. I don't think it's annoying, I think we are showing determination. Even if it isn't a prospective client but a client we already have done business with, we need to be back in front of them because they need to see we care even when there is no order, because we never know when that order will pop up. So how many sales call should we make? More than what we do now, then after that, do more on top of that.

Brandon Sanchez

I am one of the few people who would disagree that more calls can, sometimes, equal more sales. A sales person should focus on what's really important, which I believe is "what to say" when approaching a prospect. Knowing enough information of who your customer is and what their needs are and also knowing enough about your offerings and how that prospect could use your offerings will lead you to better or quality calls, not more calls. You don't want to burn your leads at inappropriate time and then have no people to call. In my opinion in better to increase the quality rather than call volume.

Yessie Narvaez

I think people get confused when they say the more calls you make the more likely you are to get more sales. Statistically yes, you would get more sales but your ratio would be down. However, I believe the concept behind the findings in the mail test, showed that making many more calls could actually help you ratio wise also, as it closes the gap between potential customers. Being from a semi-small town, people here use what they know and who they know. If you can get in and get familiar with business leaders, they will talk.

Matthew Thacker

I believe revisiting the same prospect over and over in a short period of time will produce one of two things; they will either eventually listen to what you have to say or they will tell you to leave them alone and they are not interested in you returning anymore. Either way you will know where you stand.

Lisa Lloyd

I heard a similar version of the rule of seven from my Uncle. He was the branch manager of a brokerage firm. One day, one of the brokers came to his office with a smile on his face saying he had been told "no" for the sixth time from a target client. He now felt the odds were in his favor. We all know it is a numbers game and just have to focus on feeling that familiarity of making numerous sales calls every day.

Gregg Nixon

I agree the more you are in front of a customer the more likely they are going to remember who you are. When you make 1 or 2 calls to a prospect they are more likely to forget due to the number of calls they receive each day from your competitors. If you are the one sales person that is always knocking on their door or calling them then you have a higher ratio of your name/company name sticking out in their mind.

Carla McCrea

Each time you show up, you should have you're A-game on. Because they can become familiar with the bad impression quicker than they will the good impression. Yes repeated exposure is good it usually takes several calls and visits for someone to remember your company! There is a comfort about going with the familiar product and service. We must make ourselves a name for ourselves, all the while building a strong professional reputation!

Morgan Frazier

I know about this type of selling. I once worked for a company where we were required to make 100 cold calls per day, plus take care of our regular customers and their orders. This is not an easy task but I do realize that the more calls you make the greater your chances of getting new customers.

Vickie Reihl

3. Why should you keep personal details?

Personal information about your customer is like money in the bank. Don't leave this important aspect of your business to chance.

It actually takes less time to stay well organized and to keep good records and files than it does if you are careless. There is a certain sense of satisfaction that comes from being able to find an important piece of information when it is needed.

One of the positive characteristics of a professional sales person is the pride they have in knowing everything about their customers on a personal level.

There has been a lot of money invested in lap top computers for sales people. Yet many of these computers are merely used as order entry devices. There are software programs available for keeping track of customer information, other than simply what they ordered last time. Everyone with a lap top should look into having one of these contact management programs. They can keep track of all the personal information about your customers as well as all the details of their company. When hooked up to your printer you can print 60 envelopes in less than a minute. You can write a letter and "merge" and print 60 individual letters in less than 10 minutes.

A hard copy file is just as important. This gives you a place to keep the information you want to discuss including point of sale, special presentations and information you have collected that pertains specifically to that particular customer.

Information gathering is a big part of every sales person's job. Try making a list of the top twenty most important things you should know about your customers on a personal level. Try to build a personal profile of them so you know how to deal with their personality type.

Selling any type of products without personal customer information and details will produce only average or below average results.

It is always more productive to have a method, to have your path clear. Without thinking and planning ahead it seems that trouble is always waiting for us around every corner. If your sales are not what you think they should be at this point in your career the reason is simple, you have not planned enough.

The first step is to write down your goal; the second step is to break down your goal into a series of day by day steps that will lead to the end you have in mind.

Benjamin Franklin put it this way: "By failing to prepare, you are preparing to fail".

Comments:

I have never sold a thing to a stranger, I have only sold to friends! The more you learn about your customer and the more they learn about you, the more you will grow your sales with that customer.

David Vize

When I notice in the newspaper where one of my customers is promoted or given some type of recognition I cut it out and deliver it to them with congratulations. Very effective and it is an enjoyable thing to do.

One of my customers had his company featured in an industry magazine so I had it matted and framed for him. It has been on his wall behind his desk for several years and he thanked me for it on a regular basis.

Crocker Smith

Keeping personal details about your company can assist you in showing a potential client how successful your company had become. Our company had a history page in the front of our procedures manual. When I first came to work in 2000 our office was the 14 office in the company in 3 states. As of January 2006 we had grown to 42 offices in 7 states. Now we have over 50 offices. This history page has been used to show our customer how our company has grown.

As well as knowing the personal details about your own company, it is equally important to research each potential customer that you want to sell you product or services too. The more you know about them the better chance you will have on selling your product or service that will best fit there needs, and help them become more profitable.

I had been told in the past by one of our regional VP's "That knowledge is power".

Laura Arnett

This is absolutely correct; remembering birthdays, children's names, things that your clients do in their spare time, are all great ways to take the conversation to a personal level. It is a lot easier to sell to a friend than to someone you know nothing about. On the other hand, you don't want to be looking at notes when you are talking to a client, digging for the information. So always review your notes and information on the last call you made to them before you make a new call.

Kathie Luttrell

A timely reminder that details count in every relationship. Building a database around the customer's personal interests does help whenever contact is made. I try to remember the comments about their private lives – "my wife went to Canada to see the grandchildren". When I speak to them next, I'll ask them something about the trip/grandchildren. I've lost a lot of sleep because of poor record-keeping in the office, and fully understand the need to be well-organized but it is the combined effort and cooperation of everyone that will make it work.

Paulette Clarke

You should keep personal details about your customers because it shows that you really listen to them and are thoughtful.

Let's face it, if one of your customers happened to remember that your anniversary or your birthday was coming up you would be pleasantly surprised and tend to favor that person.

Keeping personal details about your customer also helps you to work with them. Especially if they are the person who makes hiring decisions. In staffing it pays to know your customer. Some customers are more rude than others, some demand more out of their employees than others, some like people who are talkative, some hate chatterboxes...its important to keep notes on things like this so that you can adapt your sales approach and your recruiting to fit your various customers' needs and personalities.

Marquesa Ortega

It definitely feels like you have accomplished something great when you can find that important document. Being organized makes you feel better and more confident in your business and personal life. We have a computer system that allows anyone in the company to log in notes and reminders about each client which portrays that professional image when contacting clients when you say you will.

Gregg Nixon

I think it's very important to keep personal details. We keep details and notes every time we talk with someone. Not only does it help you keep track of what was said but it also serves as a reminder of what we talked about before. Maybe they had a problem a while back (nothing that you would be able to do but just a problem in general) and you ask how it worked out, they will take notice. It shows you listened and paid attention, and they'll more than likely pay you the same respect in listening to you.

Matthew Thacker

It is those little details that can make or break the sale. When we find out professional or private details about any of our clients we should us this to help us to make sales. Maybe it's remembering a birthday, and child or spouses name, or just favorite candy that can help you in the daily communication. People like to be remembered. Those little things that we say or do can make the difference because you are selling to the person not the company.

Christal Cornacchia

4. How can you control the customer's attitude?

The thing that will have the greatest effect on how you communicate with your customers is your overall attitude towards them.

When we describe a particular prospect as obnoxious, offensive, antagonistic, hard to deal with and unlikable, it is very likely they feel the same way about us. However, when we describe a customer as being friendly, likeable and easy to deal with, it is also very likely that they feel the same way about us. Who is in control? Does anyone have the power to influence the way someone responds or feels towards another person?

Have you ever heard anyone make the following comments: "There sure are a lot of hard nosed, price shoppers in our business". On the other hand, have you ever heard anyone make this comment: "There sure is a lot of nice folks in our business". They are both right.

Closer examination of these two opposite opinions will normally reveal two different attitudes towards the people they do business with. They each see their customers from their own point of view. Their own personalities are revealed in their overall attitude towards people in general.

There are very few things in sales you have complete control over, however, what you think about people is something you can control. With the right attitude towards everyone you come in contact with you can stop being your own worst enemy and have them respond favorably to you.

Customers can actually feel the negative thoughts you have about them and they are nearly impossible to hide. People can also feel the positive thoughts you have about them.

People have become less trusting of companies, or someone representing a company, trying to sell them something. Many people have been treated badly, or taken advantage of, on more than one occasion resulting in a defensive attitude. Don't let this get in your way of taking control.

Comments:

It is important to remember that even the meanest, aloof and grouchy customer has to buy from someone. Usually they know how they are. The more often you see them and interact in a positive manner, the better chance you have to sell them something. I think more often than not, deep inside they are rooting for you.

James Ruth

I have a new account, a customer very active in growing his business and very aggressive about pricing on certain specific items. He works very hard, is very scattered and requires me to be "jump-through-the-hoop" responsive to him and his needs.

I've shown him through the course of our relationship that I am willing to match him hour for hour, call for call, need for need.

He appreciates my efforts and responsiveness and has actually begun to confide in me with detailed business problems and even personal issues.

This customer actually told me when we began doing business that he would "never rely solely on one vendor" and that "your company is too small and lacking". I took that as a shot across the bow. Over the following several months of our relationship he has seen me gain access to every item he needs to run his business, be competitive in pricing with the "giants" and above all, service every need he came up with. He knows exactly what I am doing because I have repeatedly told him that my company is the only company he will ever need…and eventually will be the only company he does business with. He is actually working with me to see that happen.

The key to this customer? Essentially, I mirrored his attitude and let him see that.

Chris Chase

A salesperson is not allowed to indulge himself by displaying his negative mood or thoughts. That goes totally against the sales process. People want to feel good and if you can lift their spirits they will gravitate to you. When I approach a customer with a scowl on his face I take it as a challenge and I try to smile a lot while we are talking. Most of the time, by the end of the conversation, the person will be smiling back at me. Occasionally, there is someone who scowls more the more I smile. I usually leave at that point.

Crocker Smith

Having a bad/negative attitude can be seen by everyone; co-worker, clients, prospects. Attitude is contagious. You may go to a client and upon your arrival they may be in a bad mood, but I believe that if I am positive and upbeat, I have the power to change their day. Wouldn't you want to surround your self with people that make you feel good?

Lisa Lloyd

Going into a sales call with a positive attitude even if you like the prospect or not is always the right way to carry your presence. No matter what you think of them always let them think you are happy to be there.

Heath Blanchard

It's all about confidence! Never let them see you sweat and check your attitude at the door, even with the most miserly customer. That said, don't let them walk all over you just to appease them. You don't want to set yourself up for an abusive relationship with your customer. There is a polite way to deal with antagonistic customers. Customers will respect a salesperson who knows how to deal with difficult or negative people and/or situations in a constructive way.

Marquesa Ortega

Approaching anyone with negative thoughts is a recipe for disaster, much less a potential customer. An open-minded approach and the expectation of receiving the same, as well as good communication, assist in "controlling" most situations. The basis for any relationship is respect, and the ability to understand the reason for attitudes – positive or negative.

Paulette Clarke

Very seldom are you going to get a customer on the first try. It takes time to build a relationship and time for them to size you up as a sales person. Little things that you make small talk with the customer about go a long way. Remember their kids name and ask about the big game they mentioned the last time you spoke. It shows that you pay attention and if you pay attention to the small things they feel secure that you will pay attention to the big ones as well. It is also very relaxing to a customer and they will feel at ease with you. You can control without being controlling.

Kathie Luttrell

I agree! I feel like nobody likes a salesperson! Here is where I can run the past few lessons together! 1. You have to have a good attitude! Most likely you won't sell a thing with a bad attitude. 2. You have to make repeated visits and calls to get some name recognition, all the while presenting yourself in a positive, confident mood. 3. If you have a good attitude most of the time the prospect, cashier, server will emulate it.

Morgan Frazier

Mutual respect is what can make the difference in the business world. I know that I would have a hard time buying from someone that was negative and lacked confidence. With that being said it is difficult at times to be positive and confident. There are going to be times that as salespeople we might get down. But we need to realize that the people we are calling on aren't just buying our service, they are buying us. Do they want to buy a confident well spoken us or do they want the person that looks like they are lost. We need to not only show respect for what our customers do but we need to respect what we do. So many times we let others opinions and answers influence how we feel about our positions. Lets have respect and confidence in our positions as salespeople. If there weren't salespeople how would customers know what was available.

Brandon Sanchez

Perhaps we allow customers to walk over us because we are scared / nervous / lack the ability to show confidence and resolve and the customer is just doing his job at getting the best deal (at our expense)

I have seen where a mutual respect for one another creates a fantastic working and eventually personal relationship.

If I may draw a similarity to the bully and the timid boy in the school yard. Who does the bully go after the confident track star or the timid shy boy. If the shy boy stands up to the bully and it may become not so pretty , many times the two become best friends.

Why ....Mutual Respect

Alex McQueen

5. Why is the first minute so important?

What you do or say in that first minute of your sales presentation is more important than any other step in the sale.

A = Attention. You first must get the prospects attention with a strong statement or headline.

I = Interest. Once you have their attention you must convert it to interest. This is where you use a powerful testimonial or some relevant facts that will impact their business.

D = Details or Desire. In a sales presentation or sales letter this is where you give the details of what you are selling with the goal of arousing a desire in the prospects mind strong enough to make them want to have what you are selling.

A = Action. Here is the point that you ask them to buy.

Another way to look at this first minute is the 3 - 3 - 30 system.

You have 3 seconds to get their attention, 3 seconds to establish relevancy and 30 seconds to tell your story.

Turn and point to any person within range of your vision right now. That individual is dominated for the time being with a particular ATTITUDE. This attitude is controlling their entire personality. It is coloring their mental and emotional life. They see you through this attitude. Anything you say to them must be sifted through the screen of this fixed ATTITUDE before you can get a spark of interest in what you are talking about.

I don't think I exaggerate when I say that ninety percent of the sales you lose are mishandled in the first crucial moment. When you or I face the prospect ready to speak our first sentence we find ourselves squarely up against an attitude as closed as a barn door. What we do or say in that first sentence is more important than any other step in the sale . . . because we can't possibly sell a person who continues to retain the attitude they had before we came in.

What can we do on every call which will swing the prospects attitude so they will listen with interest to what we have to say? It's this original attitude which licks more conscientious, hard-working sales people than all of the objections in the book.

You must have an opener which breaks through that attitude and provoke the prospect to say, "Sure, I'll listen to what you have to say with an open mind. Come on in and tell your story."

What is your most successful opener? What line have you used to open your prospects mind and have them lean forward and ask for more?

Let me give you a clue. A personal example.

For seven years my company name and web site address was OrosSalesTraining.com. Business was good and I never gave it much thought. Then I began thinking about what the results were from sales people who attended my program. I started thinking about how I could find a name that represented what customers could expect.

I came up with MoreGrossProfit.com. I did a mailing AND MY BUSINESS DOUBLED OVERNIGHT! I have been offered a huge amount of money for the web site address MoreGrossProfit.com. Not a penny for OrosSalesTraining.com. hmmm!

Here is my opener... I am going to lay it on the line and tell you word for word... Let me know why you think it works and what your best opening story is.

I am not here to sell you anything, but to help you get what you want - you see, Ben, the last thing you NEED is sales training!

What you WANT is to increase your sales and exceed your plan.

You want your company to be even more successful and more profitable than it already is.

You are interested in ways to increase your gross profit so you can pay all your increasing overhead expenses, pay for the raise everyone is expecting, buy the new truck or computer, pay for the new warehouse or office building, and provide a profit to the principle owners or stock holders.

You certainly want to add new business to replace the unfortunate events that cause you to lose a customer to a competitor.

You want your sales team to be excited and motivated so they approach their territory with the positive expectations of a winner.

You want your sales team to know and use the most effective tactics and be able to play the game better than the competition.

My program will help make all those things happen. I don't sell sales training. I don't even like the words "sales training". I sell results.

Would you like to see a program that can make all those things happen?

It takes less than one minute to say!

Comments:

The best opening line that I have used is "if you listen to me for five minutes I will give you $100". Works every time but I went broke in a hurry. Seriously though, my approach is not as dependent on the first call as the follow up calls. Even if the first call is a disaster I can begin to establish credibility and familiarity so that the potential customer becomes comfortable and begins to drop their defenses.

Crocker Smith

I think the opening works because it sets the tone as, you're there for them. You're not there for your own personal gain but you want for the betterment of the buyer. I think my best opening story would have to be when after telling the potential buyer who I was, he asked, "what can I do for you." To which I responded "I'm here to find out what I can do for you." It seemed to catch him off guard and we

spoke for awhile. I think if I hadn't changed his attitude, it would have been one of those "no thanks" and you're out the door.

Matthew Thacker

How many times have we heard the expression "Don't judge a book by its cover?"

Now, how many times have we ignored it?

It's important to make your "book cover" (aka sales approach) interesting and appealing enough to get your customer to engage in your sales call. First impressions are ever important in business and in life. It's easier to uphold a good first impression than it is to overcome a bad first impression.

Marquesa Ortega

Boy, you hit the nail on the head with this one. In that first minute, you are being sized up. Do you come across professionally? Do you know what you are talking about? Is your product or service something they are already using and is what you offer better? And so on...in that first minute you want to get their attention and keep it long enough to reel them in for your sales pitch.

You won't always get their business on the first try and that is ok, but if you make a good first impression you will have more opportunities to get their business.

Kathie Luttrell

I am in the business of helping people. When you walk into a client I think what you say is different depending on the client. Never, never seem salesy. (sp) Know something about their company that will catch them off guard. This really makes you seem like you are not just there to sell something, but you are getting to know them and their company.

Danah Parmley

You only get one chance at a first impression. If you blow it in the first three seconds you can forget about the 3-3-30.

It is possible to recover from a bad first impression but it is difficult. A snazzy headline or opener is a great way to get the prospect to "lean forward and ask questions." I am selling myself to the company as you are selling more gross profit.

Morgan Frazier

My job is to make yours easier!

Lisa Lloyd

"My opener is "I am not a salesperson. I do not care about price, delivery or product. My only job is help and show you more ways to make more money". It sounds absurd but it works.

Roland DeGregorio

6. Why is your mental picture of the sale so important?

Step aside and take a look at yourself as you get out of your car prior to calling on this person we shall assume is a stranger. As you walk into the warehouse, or step into the office, your attitude will be tremendously influenced by the planning you have done before you made this call. Are you carefully prepared and organized? This is a greater confidence builder than you realize.

How strong is the inner fire of belief in what you can do for him or her? Belief in your job is reflected the moment the customer looks at you.

Is your presentation logically arranged, with all data in order, so that you can automatically put your finger on any bit of evidence?

Have you figured out in advance exactly WHAT you are going to sell... perhaps, have written the order ready for his or her signature before you go in? There's nothing like such a concrete objective to help steer your course straight from your opening to your close.

Let's take a typical case. It's Monday morning. Your prospect has spent all day Sunday looking at new automobiles and expects to buy one this week. He came in late and is two hours behind with his work. He is getting ready for a conference call. He has an appointment at eleven thirty and had placed his watch on his desk to remind him. His wife has phoned and asked him to pay the mortgage at noon. He has just interviewed three people for a job opening. His mind is a million miles away from what you have to sell. In a fraction of a second you have got to clear his mind of a thousand disturbing thoughts which are crowding into his consciousness demanding attention. The moment he lays his eyes on you, his first reaction is one of self-protection! How can he get rid of you and get back to his automobile, his bills, and the routine of the day? Yet nearly everything he buys has been sold to him by sales people who have known how to "cut through" that attitude and get attention.

What is your mental picture of this customer or prospect? Do you feel he or she is your superior and that you are liable to be a little embarrassed in their presence?

Get this mental picture right in your mind before making the call and the results will speak for themselves. Don't assume they are going to be eager to see you come through the door - be prepared.

Be mentally prepared! Just because they are not going to be eager to see you does not mean that you can't be eager to see them. It's all in your mind.

What if you received word that you inherited $500,000 just moments before you were going to see this person? Would you act more positive? Would you be excited? YES! You would probably make the sale without a hitch.

Then, after your appointment, you found out it was a mistake and you only inherited $500.

Don't wait for an inheritance - it's not coming.

Thinking right towards people means filling your mind with good thoughts about everyone and eliminating all negative thoughts. Every day say to yourself; "this is going to be the best day I have ever had." Before every sales call say to yourself; "this is going to be the best sales call I have ever made". In silence and to yourself say; "I really like you" when dealing with your clients or preparing to meet with a customer. Do the same when approaching a stranger or new customer. They will feel what you are thinking and it will be impossible for them not to like you in return. The right attitude towards people is a powerful tool. Use this tool to overcome any self limiting feelings when talking to an individual or a group. This positive attitude towards people will help you reach your sales objective faster than anything else you do.

Comments:

I strongly believe the keys to any good sales adventure is planning, organizational skills, rehearsing, focus, and a positive outlook. Without anyone of these techniques it could cause a sale to be lost. It's not about perfectionism it's about putting your all into what you do. I always say never half step anything you do. Practice until its time to accept your Oscar; actors and actress's know this well.

Shawn Hollis

Bob, you really nailed it on this one. I read it three times and I think this is one of your most critical lessons to succeeding in the sales business.

Crocker Smith

Your attitude influences everything you do. Keep positive attitude because is reflects in you body language and facile expressions. Make sure your presentation is arranged properly so that you can answer any question that the client may have. Picture what you want to say before you go into a meeting. Fill your mind with good thoughts and eliminate any negative ones. Keeping positive attitude and appearance, and always be prepared.

Laura Arnett

This is excellent advice. I especially like the part about going in feeling like you have just inherited a large sum of money, because if you sell enough you will, it's called a bonus!!

Kathie Luttrell

As with the customer having a million things racing through their mind, sales people do as well. I feel it is important to clear your mind prior to making a sales presentation or having any discussion with a current or potential client. It has been driven into me by a prior boss that staying focused on the task at hand & erasing the distractions causes by personal, business, coworkers, family etc…will produce results. Allowing outside interferences distract you will only cost you the sale and ability to achieve your goal. Painting a positive picture & clearing your mind prior to walking in will give you the extra boost & confidence which will felt by the prospect

Carla McCrea

Having a smile on your face when you enter a sales call means a lot. Being positive no matter what. We know people have a negative feeling towards sales people automatically but if we enter the meeting with a winning attitude, it can be very contagious.

Kimberly Burgess

I think having a positive mental picture when going into a sales call. It must also be genuine, because people can feel when you are putting on false enthusiasm. Walking in and not having that positive mental picture will more than likely lead to you not even breaking into their attention span. As a sales person your goal is to help people by servicing them the product that can best fit their needs. If you're not enthusiastic about what you're there for, people will see that. People want to be helped by people who want to help, not the ones that make it out to be a chore.

Matthew Thacker

I work with different sales people all the time. You know right away who are the ones who are successful and those who are just struggling along. I do not walk in to most circumstances with a game plan. I once was with a sales person who said he just wanted to see a customer to say hello. I told him he could do that on the phone, without me. We then change course and set a plan of topics and ideas for the customer and walked in.

I am sure it was better than saying hello.

Roland DeGregorio

You should always be mentally prepared to make a sales call. If you prepare yourself mentally and plan ahead for the sales call, then the sales call will be a lot easier and a lot more relaxing for you the sales person and also for the customer or prospective client. You should always eliminate the negative thoughts about a sales call and fill

your mind with the good thoughts. If you have to pump yourself up by saying to yourself that this is going to be the best sales call that you have ever made. Having a positive attitude will help you to reach your sales objective faster.

Amy G. Harrell

Getting in the right state of mind before visiting a possible client or a current customer can make the difference in making the sale or getting an additional order. A positive attitude will help in putting you in the right state of mind. Tell your self that you like this person and believe is and it will shine through. Also be prepared wither it is a routine call or a new sales lead. Having confidence in yourself because you know that you are prepared will also be reflected in your actions and conversation when you are in front of the customer or client.

Christal Cornacchia

Painting a positive mental picture is very important when making a sale. If you walk into a sales meeting feeling insecure about yourself you will not sell anything. The client will sense your negative feelings and have severe reservations about putting his faith in you and your products. If you walk into a meeting feeling great about yourself and your job you are much more likely to have a positive outcome. Thinking positively will help you on a much broader scale than just sales. If you are a positive person your life will seem much easier than a negative person's life. Nothing comes easy in this world, but the more positive you are the better quality of life you will experience.

Cullin Hamm

7. Why are personal questions so important?

Many people are deeply involved in things other than their business. They usually have something in their office that is like an open invitation to ask about it. Many sales people avoid talking about these things because they think it is too obvious, however, just the opposite is true. People attach a great deal of importance to the things in their life other than their work. They add to their overall self image and talking about them gives them a great deal of satisfaction.

We find people interesting because of our similiarities not our differences. This method of bonding is very powerful - finding something you have in common with your customer or prospect. Whether you were both in the military, lottery winners or both like playing golf, look for things you have in common and you will become instant friends.

Years ago I was at a mall in Chicago with some time to kill and I saw an encyclopedia booth set up with a display of their books. I didn't want to sit through a sales pitch, however, I did want to know how much it cost on a CD. I approached the sales person and asked for the price. He responded with a question; "What kind of work do you do?" That was all it took. For the next hour we engaged in a conversation about training and if it wasn't for my wife, who came and bailed me out, I might have been the owner of something I had no intention of buying.

How did he get me so involved in talking for an entire hour? He did it by asking personal questions. Questions that I was delighted to answer.

Never hesitate to ask about their family if there is a picture, their golf score if there is a trophy, their hunting adventures, favorite fishing spots, backpacking experience, etc.

What do people like to talk about? Here's a clue. The psychology department at a leading university recently did a test to determine what people do or think. When 500 women were given a fountain pen and asked to write something, 92 percent wrote their own names first. When shown twelve monthly calendars, 470 out of 500 women looked at their own birth date first. When 500 men were shown a map of the country 447 looked first at the location of their home town.

Here are the results of another study done by two professors of psychology in an effort to find out what the average person talks about. They listened in on 500 casual conversations at restaurants, theatre lobbies, stores, barber shops and other places where people meet. They found that people in New York talk about the same things as people in Ohio or California. In 49 percent of the cases men were talking about business, 14 percent about sports, and 13 percent about other men. With women 22 percent of the conversations were about men, 19 percent about clothes, and 15 percent about other women. In general it was found that men talk about things, while women are more interested in talking about people.

Comments:

I called on a potential customer who controlled purchasing for a large company. He was all business and did not want to talk to me about anything else. This went on for a couple of years without him giving me any business. One night at my son's school basketball game I noticed that he was a referee. I could not wait to go see him the next day. Sure enough, we had our longest meeting so far talking about sports and slowly I began to have success selling to him.

Occasionally I have experienced customers who just want to talk about themselves to anyone who will listen and have no interest in a two way conversation. That is no fun.

Crocker Smith

I totally agree with this lesson. Developing a sincere interest in your customers it's very important in order to build trusting relationships with them. Believe it or not small details are important in any type of relationships. People remember you for little things that may look insignificant to other people, but impressing for others. Amaze your customers, make them feel that you are not there just to get an order, but because you truly care about them. Without customers, you won't have a business. I believe that getting personal means recognizing each customer's unique needs and responding to them.

Yessie Narvaez

I think asking about things that they are interested in gets them to let there guard down, which in turn leads to what it is you want to talk about. Listen to what it is they are saying and you'll pick up what it is they need from you.

Brian Spraggins

I think this is very true. Each person we speak with is very different from the next. We need to look at every angle in order for them to become comfortable and want to continue a conversation with us. Some are all business, but others want to talk about something else. I feel that if someone didn't want to talk about something then they would not have it out in plain view for everyone to see. I have always been taught that if they are displaying it then they want to talk about it. If there is a trophy out, ask about it, odds are they are going to enjoy telling you the story about how they won that trophy. People also like talking about themselves if given the opportunity.

Brandon Sanchez

Personal questions are so important because people like to talk about what they do outside of work. Asking about someone's personal interest can be their distraction during the normal commotion of hectic business. I personally like to ask about someone's golf game if they have anything golf related in their office. It seems to be a great door opener.

Matthew Thacker

For me it is so much easier to go to a client or prospect and strike up a conversation about something on a personal level rather than jumping straight to business. It seems to set a more receptive environment too. The person you're speaking with has a tendency to let their guard down against "the sales person" if you can start the conversation on a personal level.

Lisa Lloyd

I was at a party last weekend and talking to other guys about their business is the best topic of conversation to break the ice. Everybody works so you know that would be a common interest and a passion. Not that my main objective at a party is setting a meeting, but it sets the tone for a relaxed playing field. As is the same when asking what the story is behind that special picture or trophy. It sets the tone for a relaxed atmosphere and a friendly meeting.

Gregg Nixon

Business can be like dating. It's important you get the "scoop" on prospective clients before you enter a relationship with them, and conversely it is important they learn everything they need to know about you and your business as well.

You will need to ask personal questions and take good notes of the way your client works, what their environment/organizational culture is like, what drives their business and the different types of personalities you'll be working with so that you can adjust and adapt to best serve their needs.

Marquesa Ortega

This is so true. I was recently closing a deal and while in the Manager's Office I commented on his décor. He mentioned that his wife had done the decorating and during the conversation I realized that I knew his wife. We talked for an additional 30 minutes and I left feeling much more comfortable than I had before, because now our relationship had become personal. And each time I go to see him I will have something I can talk with him about besides just business.

Kathie Luttrell

About the author Bob Oros

Regardless of whether you are reading one of his books or attending one of his programs, the most frequent comment is: "This guy has been there, he is one of us, I am going to use these strategies."

With over 2,000 speaking engagements in all 50 states and several international locations for manufacturers, distributors and associations, you can be sure you will get the results and information you are looking for. Prior to starting his speaking career, Bob served six years in the US Navy as a Communications Specialist and then worked his way from a street sales person to the position of National Sales Manager for a Fortune 200 company.

Bob has received awards for speaking, writing and marketing too numerous to mention.

Additional Topics by Bob Oros

Why Sales People Fail

The Key to Selling Anybody

The Power of Expectations

Add Value to Every Product

How to Justify Your Price

Lost in 60 Seconds

One Good Reason to Buy

Control a Buyer's Attitude

How to Create Demand

Smoke Screen Objections

Take the Risk Out of Sales

How Small Companies Get Big